50 Streams of Income

Shonda Miles

For more information on Shonda Miles, go to www.shondamiles.com. Shonda Miles offers a range of Products and Services including Multiple Streams of Income-how to make money while you sleep and How to make an extra $100,000 this year.

Other books by Author

10 Ways to Write an EBook in 10 days

101 Success Questions that will change your life

Remote Medical Coding Jobs

Tips for Staring an Online Business

How to Love Your Spouse again

How to Double Your Income in 12 Months or less

50 Tips to Jumpstart Your Success

50 Streams of Income

How to Get the Job You Want

21 Ways to Start a Marriage off Right

18 Ways to Break into Coding

21 Ways to make a Blended Family Work

I am

Marty learns to swim

30 days to being a better Christian

How to create an audio product

Table of Contents

Introduction

In Money: Master the Game, Anthony Robbins says "No matter where you live, if you don't have another source of income, you could end up the best-dressed greeter at Wal-Mart."

Multiple Streams of Income. Get Multiple Streams of Income. Hurry & Get Multiple Streams of Income. If you don't do anything else for the rest of your life Get Multiple Streams of Income.

Multiple streams of income are the smart way to secure your future. It is a lot of work on the front end but it is peace of mind on the backend.

Of course there are no guarantees in life. I can't guarantee you will make money with any of these. The time will pass anyway so it won't hurt to cultivate some of these.

If you want to make more money in the long term you can. If you want to make more money you are going to have to do a whole lot of things you've never done before.

Some of it will make you uncomfortable. Some of it, you just won't want to do. Successful people do what unsuccessful people don't want to do. As the economy continues to change, it is necessary to develop multiple streams of income.

The key is to pick one and learn about it. If it doesn't interest you, then move on to something else.

Jim Rohn said "If you want things to change, you have to change."

Diversifying your Income Streams leads to Increased Wealth.

"Take up one idea and act on it. Make that one idea your life. Think of it, dream of it, and live on that idea. Let the brain, muscles, nerves, and every part of your body be full of that idea and leave all other ideas alone. This is the way to success."

"Allow yourself to dream and fantasize about your ideal life; what it would look like, and what it would feel like. Then do something every day to make it a reality!" Brian Tracy

Take massive action

"The path to success is to take massive determined action." Anthony Robbins

"You are successful the moment you start moving toward a worthwhile goal." Charles Carlson

"If I have correct goals and I keep pursing them the best way I know how, everything falls into line. If I do the right thing, I am going to succeed." Dan Dierdorf

"The great end of life is not knowledge, but action." Thomas Henry Huxley

"If you have goals and procrastination you have nothing. If you have goals and you take action, you will have anything you want." Thomas J. Villord

Why I wrote this book

I wrote this book so anyone who wants to increase their income they can. It is no longer "Knowledge is power," but it is what you do with that Knowledge that is power.

I wrote this book because I am a believer in having multiple streams of income. If you lose your job or illness affects your family, the way it did mine in 2015 how will you take care of your family?

In 2015, I had a baby that was born with tracheomalacia. She received a trach at 4 weeks old. She stayed in the hospital for 2 weeks. I didn't work for 3 months. Without the income for 3 months, it proved to be almost catastrophic for my family. This changed my life forever.

After this, I started to pay attention to tragedy or illness happening to families all around me. These families or at least one person in the family needed to be off to take care of the loved one but needed to still provide for his or her family. How can they do this unless they cultivate Multiple Streams of Income before they actually needed it?

The important thing is to create as many passive streams of income as possible. You want to make money while you sleep. No, I am not advocating a get rich scheme. What I am saying is you want to have more than one stream of income coming into your account each month. If one stream dries up, you have something else. This is the true way to wealth.

If you have ever went without income or had to be without income due to the illness of a family member or your own, this will certainly resonate more with you. If you haven't, you have time to prepare in case it does.

None of us are indispensable. We can lose our job tomorrow. We could lose our ability to work in the blink of an eye. Cultivating Multiple Streams of Income is a win-win for you. You can secure your future in that you can know you can have income whether you are working as an employee or running your business in Hawaii.

There are only so many hours in a day which means there is only so many hours you can work in a day. The only way to leverage your time is to create passive income. At some point you will be able to do what you want when you want.

Cultivating Multiple streams of income is not easy. It takes hard work- a lot of it. It also means you will have to learn things you might not know now. It will be so worth it to you in the long run.

This list is in no way exhaustive. I hope it will get the creative juices flowing. I hope this book is in a long list of books you intend to read about increasing your income and making more money.

One of my favorite books is *One Minute Millionaire*. The authors are Mark Victor Hansen and Robert G Allen. This book changed my life. I am able to see opportunities where I didn't see them before. Of course I have read hundreds of books since then but it was certainly a great start to changing my mindset. If you haven't read it consider reading it right away.

Passive income is important because it will add income to your bottom line without you having to work over and over to get a paycheck. An example could be money you earn from rental income, from writing a book or from dividends. It is considered passive income if you do not have to be totally active in earning it. That does not mean you will not spend any time earning it, but the amount of time that you do spend will be much less than your full-time job.

No matter which of these streams you choose, do some of the following as part of the research. Read the top 10 books in your niche. Read articles on the top 10 blogs in your niche. Listen to the top 10 podcasts in your niche. Read the top 10 forums in your niche.

1. Web designer-Create Websites. Become a Website Designer. Web designers create websites for small business owners or solopreneurs. The key word here is they design which means they have to place images in ideal spaces. They have to break up the text. They are the expert and have to be able to advice clients on what works best You can niche down and create websites for certain types of businesses such as service businesses only or Coaches or Authors or whatever you choose. No you don't have to be a web designer. You can be up and running in no time. You don't need to know to read html code. You don't need to know how to write html code. It helps to be a little creative in order to make the website you are designing look it's best. Consider studying 100 or more websites to get the feel for how sites look and are designed. Most websites are designed using Word Press. It is easy. It is fast to use. You can use YouTube or UDemy as a Quick start tutorial on WordPress. Of course a website designer must have a great website. Website Designers can command $2,000-$5000 per website or more. You can also offer cheaper services for basic website design for work that takes 30 minutes or less. I like this because if you can use Word then you can use Word Press to design websites. Hint: You can outsource this and collect the profits. A web designer is worth its weight. If you choose this one realize you are offering a valuable service to your clients. Web designers should understand domain registration, hosting and building websites. 50 Free Books for Web Designers & Developers
https://speckyboy.com/2015/01/12/free-web-design-ebooks-2014/.

2. SEO Consulting-With all the websites coming online they will need SEO (search engine optimization) services. If you have an online business, this is certainly worth learning. SEO is basically how search engines list you in the search engines based on keywords on your website. Keywords are words your customers will use to find you. It is important to know the keywords your potential customers will use to try to find you or solve their problems. While businesses know that this is one of the keys to their online success. Most companies do it poorly. If a business is not on page 1 or 2 on Google chances are they won't be found for those keywords. You can start with those on Page 5 or 6 and further back and create a plan to target them to help them with their search engine optimization. Of course you have to be on Page 1 of Google yourself. There are great courses on Udemy on this as well. It is necessary to understand client's target market, their pain, problem and the solutions you will offer. Google Keyword Planner tool will be your friend.

3. Social Media Marketing Consulting-Do you love Social Media? Do you find that you spend a lot of time on Social Media? If so Social Media Consulting may be right for you. Most small business owners don't have time to do this. Hint: You can outsource all of the work. Check out Retortal. You can hire a VA (Virtual assistant) to do this for you. You can find one on Fiverr.com, Guru, Upwork or Iwriter.com. Some of the responsibilities include posting blog post, making post on Facebook, Twitter, LinkedIn, Instagram, Blab, Periscope, Content Marketing Strategy creation and developing a Social Media Strategy. The more of these you are familiar with the better. The

higher your following the better. In order to be successful here you will need to be able to help create engaging content.

4. Amazon Kindle-I love Amazon Kindle. It is passive income. I make money while I sleep. I do the work once and I make money over and over. There is strength in numbers though. What I mean here is the more books you write for Amazon Kindle the more money you will make. You can write the books for Amazon Kindle or you can outsource it to someone on Iwriter, Upwork or Guru.com. If you decide to write the book yourself, it helps to choose a topic you know a lot about. You can then record yourself talking into your phone. You can have an e-book for Amazon Kindle in an hour. You can publish your book for free with Amazon Kindle and reach millions of readers. However, it is best to have someone else create a great book cover as well as format book for you. Books that are 8,000-15,000 have become the norm for the short Kindle book.

You can earn royalties of 70% of book price as long as it is at least $2.99. Your book will be available for sell to customers in the U.S., U.K, Germany, and many more countries.

Amazon Kindle makes publishing easy and fast. It takes less than 5 minutes. Your book will usually show up on Amazon in less than 48 hours.

5. Amazon FBA-Fulfillment services by Amazon. You have your products shipped to Amazon's warehouse and they take care of everything else. They handle the purchase, shipping, customer service, and returns. You can't beat

that. You can order Products wholesale thru Alibaba. It is free to sign up for an Alibaba account. Order samples to test the quality of the products. You can start small and test several products. The key is to try products that are light weight and inexpensive. There are great courses on Udemy on this. Of course there are short books on Amazon Kindle as well. You get one month free as a Professional as a seller on Amazon. You can sell a few products or a lot. Of course, you will be running a business. Be sure you have a business license, EIN, etc to run a legitimate business. Amazon has over 95 million unique visitors a month.

6. Affiliate Marketing-Affiliate marketers are those who receive a commission or referral fee for recommending a product for a business. You will have to promote the product in order to make any money. Check out Clickbank.com, 1ShoppingCart, Amazon or CommisionJunction.com for more information. To find out if your favorite company has an affiliate program, scroll down to the bottom of the page and look for Affiliate or Referral program. This is usually where beginners start. In order to promote someone else product consider writing a series of articles to promote your affiliate product. You want to be an expert on that niche so you can promote products. Write reviews on products you recommend. Always let your customers or potential customers know you will make money if they buy the product. Before recommending a product always try to use it first. So you can be sure you are recommending a great product. Affiliate commissions can be as high as 75%. When you decide to become an affiliate, you will sign up with that company to become an affiliate. Once you sign up to become an affiliate you

will receive a unique id and or website that will allow you to be paid for the products or services you recommend.

7. Freelance Writing-Become a Freelance Writer. Do you like writing? Can you stick to Deadlines? Create your own website offering your services. Read books on Writing. Read every day and Write every day. Create a schedule. Don't let anything keep you from doing this. You will get better at writing every day. Consider purchasing Michael Masterson's Get it Done CD. It is $10 but a great motivator and great resources. Visit Wealthy Web Writer and The Write Life, Writers Digest and Writer'slife.org for additional information. Writers.com is the first writers school online offers a host of writing classes for fiction and nonfiction authors. The Content Authority is a freelance writing site. Customer support handles everything. They pay you .25 a word.

8. Copywriting-Copywriting is basically the written word often called text that sells like hotcakes. "A copywriter is a salesperson behind a typewriter" says Judith K. Charles. It has people taking out their credit card ready to buy. If interested check out AWAI Six Figure Copywriting program. Also read *The Copywriter's Handbook* written by Robert W. Bly.

9. Webinars-Webinars are a great way to sell your knowledge. More and more businesses are finding out just how lucrative this is. You can do one of two models. The first is you can offer a free webinar thru Facebook ads. Have a budget in mind. Start small. At the end of a great webinar full of valuable

content you can offer a single service such as Bootcamp, Coaching, Teleseminar. The second one is offer a 60 or 90-minute webinar for a price. You can also sell a Bootcamp this way as well. You will need a list that you have built a relationship with. People are going to test your content (free content) out before they buy from you. The secret to great presentations is Graphic River. They have great presentation templates for under $25. They are typically $10-$20. This will make you look like an instant professional. All you have to do is provide the text and some images and you are good to go. Lewis Howes makes at least $6,000 per hour doing webinars. While others make $30,000 or more per webinar. With a webinar, you can basically use your outline as your slides. Images are essential. Follow up is crucial here. Without proper follow up, you could be leaving a lot of money on the table.

10. Teleseminars- Teleseminars are great! They are just that-seminars over the phone. They are anywhere from 60 to 90 minutes at a time. The key is providing handouts before call. You can use a free service for calls such as freeconferencecall.com or freeconferencecalling.com. They are both free. You can also use instantteleseminar.com. You can talk directly from an outline vs. with a webinar, you have to have graphics/images for your presentation.

11. Real Estate Investing-Become a Real Estate Investor. Real Estate Investing has made a lot of people wealthy. It is a wealth creation tool. It is used by most people to grow wealth. It provides financial independence to those who take advantage of it. There are all types of ways to structure a deal with no money down. I would advise getting your finances in order if this is one of the streams of income you want to cultivate. Increase your credit score by getting a free credit report from annualcreditreport.com. Pay down debt quickly using Dave Ramsey's The total Money Makeover. Make saving a habit. Start with as much as you can save and then increase to 10% quickly. Increase to 20% after that. Eliminate all unnecessary expenses. This is your future. Visit biggerpockets.com. This is a forum that provides a ton of information on real estate investing for free. You can meet other investors and ask questions. Go to www.reiclub.com to attend a Real Estate Investing meeting in your area. The fee is nominal. It will give you the opportunity to meet other real estate investors as well as learn more about real estate investing. Educating yourself, Learning from your mistakes and taking action are key here.

12. Real Estate Wholesaling-Learn about Real Estate Wholesaling. Real Estate Wholesaling is basically you are the middleman between another Real Estate investor (buyer) and the seller of the property. Wholesalers tend to make $6,000 to $10,000 per transaction. You can get started regardless of credit and whether you have any money or not. "Wholesaling is selling a contract not real estate." Wholesaling is more about marketing a property than about real estate. You have to find a property that is below market value (distressed) that with a little work sometimes a lot of work can be sold for a

big profit. Consider purchasing *Wholesaling Real Estate* by Brent D. Driscoll. It is a great resource. I also like *Wholesale Bible* by Than Merrill. Build relationships with real estate agents, other real estate investors, private money lenders etc, Know your area (target area where you will be buying properties). You will need systems in place to run your business more effectively. Read *The EMyth Real Estate Investor* written by Michael E. Gerber, Than Merrill and Paul Esajian for more information on systems. This book is exceptional. Be sure to have a follow up system in place so nothing falls thru the cracks. The key here is building a business that will run without you. I love to use McDonald's as an example here. If you go to a McDonalds in Japan or New York they are run the same. They make hamburgers the same way. If you google REI Club underneath reiclub.com you will see where you click the link and read free books and audio.

13. Network Marketing-Companies such as Mary Kay, Avon, Primerica are considered Network Marketing companies. They provide great training. You can build great relationships as well. If you choose this one make sure you read about sales, building relationships, building teams and leadership.

14. Coaching-There are all types of Coaches. There are Health coaches, Business coaches, Marketing Coaches, Relationship Coaches, Career Coaches, Spiritual Coaches, Sales Coaches, Executive Coaches, Life Coaches and on and on. "Professional Coaching brings many wonderful benefits, fresh perspectives on personal challenges interpersonal effectiveness and increased confidence. And the list does not end there." ICF

"Coaching benefits your clients by helping them identify the goals and dreams that will bring them real lasting happiness. It also helps them remove the obstacles, limitations and circumstances that are holding them back from those those dreams, and it shows them how to make their ideal life a reality." Mary Morrissey

A Coach usually has some type of training or certification. As of this writing there is no governing body for Coaches which means there are people getting a business license and calling themselves a coach with no formal training. If you want to be in business for a long time and really help people some type of training is needed. International Coaching Federation is popular for offering coaching certification. You can google the Coaching you are interested in and type training or certification behind it. Also Read Anyone can Coach by Sean Mize. You can coach people all over the world over the phone. In order to be a good coach you must be a good listener with good analytical skills. In Coaching Clues, Marian J Their says "A coach is not a business partner, therapist, buddy, or confidant. The coaching relationship is a negotiated partnership in which all parties must respect each other and remain committed to the boundaries of a professional relationship. Small changes can make a huge difference." A business coach (specializing in small business) can prove to be very beneficial. A business coach can often help you catapult your success (business) to next level in a short period of time. A business coach is often a sounding board, an accountability partner, a cheerleader someone committed to your success. A business coaches main goal is to help you to be successful. This happens because they provide expertise in areas you are struggling with. They often can help you figure out what is holding you back. They can suggest small incremental changes that can make a big difference.

15. Consulting-Consulting is a great industry to help people in their business solve their problems. There are all types of Management consulting including Strategy Consulting, Operations Consulting, IT Consulting, HR Consulting. Read books by Alan Weiss. He tells you how to do everything from how to get started to pricing to marketing.

"The Question Is The Answer. Listen to your clients when they state their problems. A good consultant will often hear the answer in how a problem is presented, and this is a great skill to acquire." -Carlos Alvarenga

16. Blogging-You can start a blog with Wordpress.org rather inexpensively. You will need a domain (godaddy.com) and hosting (bluehost.com). This is less than $50 to start. The domain is a yearly expense. The hosting is monthly or you can pay yearly. You can choose a topic or niche and start writing consistently on that topic. Think about solutions you can offer to your potential customers. Think value. Blogging is a great way to add to your income. You can review other's products and use an affiliate link for the products you like. You can also blog about your own products or services. You can blog about 7 Myths regarding your niche or 7 Mistakes your target market often makes regarding your niche.

17. Membership Sites-You can start with 4 hours of content and add it to weekly Membership site are great continuous income. You can use Word press plugin -password protected. You can use Wishlist Member to start your membership site. It is $197 developer license. Other Membership site options include aMember, Digital Access Pass, Kajabi, Nanacast, Optimize Member and S2Member Pro. "According to Dr. Jeanette Cates, a respected Internet marketing strategist and leading authority on membership sites, there are several types of membership sites you will want to consider; a) Interview sites, where you interview an expert each month and offer it to your members for a monthly fee. b) Teaching sites, where you offer teleseminar or webinar trainings on your topic, both live and recorded. c) Digital download delivery sites, where your content is protected behind your secure membership site location d) Training sites, where you can offer training to your team members and staff e) Sites where you can accumulate your own articles, e-books, short reports, and other content and sell access to

it on a monthly or annual fee basis. Membership content might include videos, interviews, articles, short reports and/or teleconferences.

18. Virtual Summit-Virtual Summits seem to be a hot thing now. Basically you can get experts together usually 15 or more about 35 is the most I have seen. Each expert can speak on related topic for about 40 minutes. They give a free gift at the end to build their list. The experts get exposure as well. The Virtual Summit is free to attend live. The organizer can usually charge a fee for customers to receive the recordings, PDF transcripts, and other free gifts.

19. Premium Packages (Gold, Silver, Platinum)-You can offer these packages for Coaching. You can offer these as tiers for a Membership sites. People like options. This will reduce the number of people you will lose to the higher price. Of course as you go up in price the customers get more value. As you go do in price the customer loses something. You want to capture those people who can pay more for more services as well as not leave money on the table for those who want what you have to offer but can't afford the higher cost right now.

20. Bootcamp-A boot camp is usually a webinar or teleseminar series over 4 to 8 weeks teaching something. It can be live or recorded. It is usually $497 to $1997 depending on perceived value of content.

21. EBook-see Amazon Kindle. This is similar to Amazon Kindle except you can sell this on your website. Ebooks are a growing trend. You don't need a Kindle to buy and read books on Kindle.

22. Interview Series-Interview series is where you will interview several people on related topics. You can then sell it.

23. Home Study Course see Bootcamp. You can turn a Bootcamp into a home study course. Home Study courses are super easy to create. You will be surprised at how many people will invest in your course. Everyone wants the convenience -to learn at their own convenience. You can create a digital or a Physical copy of your Home Study Course. If you create a digital copy you can get someone to create a box, CD, Binder of what your course will look like if they received it in the mail by outsourcing it to Guru.com or Fiverr. Of course you can do the same thing for the Physical Copy. You will have to add in the cost of creating the Binder cover, spine and back as well as the cost of the binder and copies. If you have actual CD's or DVD's you will have to add that cost in as well. You could offer the physical and digital with the Physical being more. The customer will also incur shipping cost. If the customer purchased the physical, you may want to consider giving them the digital copy for free so they can access it right away. In order to create the Home Study Course you will create your outline first and then start filling in the holes.

24. Home Study Manual-You can have the Home Study Course transcribed, add action items, checklists and you will have a Home Study Manual.

25. Live Seminars-See Live Workshop. Live Seminars and Live Workshops are often used interchangeably but they do have subtle differences. A Live Workshop could be more activity based where participants will be expected to complete several activities with a lot of interaction whereas for the Live Seminar-it maybe more lecture based with minimal interaction.

26. Create a Mastermind Group-Mastermind Group is a group of like-minded individuals coming together to help each other with challenges. It is usually less than 8 people to one group. The meetings are anywhere from 60-90 minutes long biweekly or monthly. If you decide to create mastermind groups consider joining one as well to see how it works. The investment people are willing to pay is anywhere from $97 a month to $20,000 a year. Yes, you read that right. What you will receive from a mastermind group is invaluable. Make sure your customers know that. It is like a having a fresh set of eyes on a problem you are too close to see a solution for. Visit passionforbusiness.com. Karyn Greenstreet does a great training on this. Participants tend to see remarkable results as members of the group hold each other accountable weekly or biweekly for the goals they have set.

27. Ecourse-An ecourse is a course by email. It can be dripped through email the actual lesson or you can send them a link where it would take them to your site to consume the lesson. You can do this through your Autoresponder. An autoresponder is an email management software that houses the emails of your customers and allows you to email as you wish. You can make this lesson a short video with an Assignment or action item. You also can offer some handouts or checklist as well. You can offer a shorter course for free and then upsell participants or you can sell them the regular course. Ideally you want to send participants an email each day with a link taking them to your site for the lesson. This will give you traffic to your site. Of course you can provide the lesson to them right in the email. It is totally up to you.

28. Coaching DIY-You can create lessons to help someone do something. You can provide it as a recording only. Customers can buy it and listen and consume at their leisure. You can do 12 lessons or 8 lessons or however many you thing necessary to solve the customer's problem. Consider offering more than one modality such as Audio, PDF transcript and Video. You can do a lesson a week or biweekly or every 10 days. This might be worth testing to see the increments that work best. Sometimes weekly is too much for busy professionals. Ideally you want to upsell them to something else at the end of this coaching. You always want to be thinking about how to move customers along your funnel to optimize sales.

29. Virtual classes-Virtual classes are classes online. You can teach classes for online schools on your area of expertise. You can create your own classes as well and offer them on your website. You can keep it short and sweet-60 minutes. You can teach class or offer a series of classes. You can create a Certification program where participants would have to take 8 or 9 classes to get a certification. Just do one class at a time. But think in terms of creating several classes or having an entire program at some point.

30. Books (print) Write one page a day. Aim for 1,000 words a day. In 60 days you will have a book done. Stay focused and you can do it. Be sure to start with an Outline. Read on your topic as often as you need to preferably daily. It will reduce writers block. While books alone don't take to make a lot of money, you can use your book as a platform for other things. For example, a keynote speaker or creating a course based on your book. Books give you credibility. People see you as an expert when you write a book. After all you would have spent hours to write that book while also sharing your years of experience. Most people know it takes a great deal of persistence and discipline to complete a book. Most people go their whole lives wanting to write a book but never actually doing it.

31. Teach at a local University-Teach a class on your local university. If you have a topic that the school may be interested in offering the community contact the Continuing Education department and they can tell you the process. You can also Google the school and on their website search for Continuing education department. They will provide the information there on whether you need to submit a Proposal or a simple one sheet with what you will teach and what students will learn. I am sure there are several subjects you could easily teach and share your experiences with students. Be careful that you teach something you want to be known for. Teach something you are passionate about and know well.

32. Prep for Certification-Have you completed a certification that most people are struggling to pass? Can you teach your techniques to others? Can you provide a home study course or manual to help others? This one is often overlooked but it can be a great source of income. If you create an Information product like an e-book or video series, you can create it once and put it on your website. This way people can purchase anytime and consume it at their leisure and you won't have to do anything else except update regularly. You always want to provide products like this in several modalities to cover different learning styles. Some people want to read an eBook while others want to listen by way of mp3 download and yet others will want to see and hear it through a webinar.

33. Etsy-Are you good with crafts? Are you creative? Visit etsy.com for more information. You can sell your crafts on Etsy. With more than 54 million registered members and over US$195 million in annual revenue it's safe to say they're an eCommerce giant. Look at what the big guys are doing and try to do it better.

34. Create an App-You can outsource this to Guru.com or Upwork.com if you have an idea. You would just need to post what you want being very clear on what you want the end product to be and see if someone can create it for you.

35. Create software- You can outsource this to Guru.com or Upwork.com if you have an idea. You would just need to post what you want being very clear on what you want the end product to be and see if someone can create it for you. You can also buy license to sell other people's on JVZoo.com.

36. Real Estate Agent-Real Estate Agents usually make $3,000 or more per house depending on where you live and how much the purchase price of the house is. This is also a great way to get into Real Estate Investing. You will have to take a Real Estate Class and pass an exam for your state. You can usually take the Real Estate class at your local community college. Consider talking with several Real Estate agents already in the business to see how they got started, startup cost and what they recommend. Some real estate offices in your area may offer free Real Estate Training. There are some startup costs as well usually less than $6,000 depending on where you live. This cost usually includes MLS (Multiple Listing) Software. This is how Agents find houses for their clients as well as list their client's houses. It is important to be able to build relationships.

37. Insurance Sales-There are all types of Insurance you could sell. From life insurance to health insurance and everything in between. Usually a property and Casualty (P & C) license is required. Check your state requirements.

38. Keynote Speaking-If you like to talk-this may be for you. Read books on Speaking. Prepare your message. Craft your story. What lessons have you learned? What can you tell people that will them? Study your favorite speakers. Record yourself audio and video and listen and watch yourself. This will be helpful for improving. Join Toastmasters and National Speaker's Association (your local chapter). Ask your peers for constructive feedback.

39. Live Workshop-Create a program where you teach people something you know. You can invite guest to speak or you can speak the whole day. You can do this 4 hours or 8 hours. You can do this in a Hotel Conference room. Make it interactive. Try to get people to implement right away what they are learning. Make sure activities are fun and useful. Put participants into groups. Use icebreaker activities. Use handouts to reinforce material taught. Provide notes with Key points on it so participants can really focus on learning material being taught in Workshop.

40. Become a Freelancer-Freelancing includes writing, website design, search engine Optimization and social media marketing and a host of other things. Check out Guru.com, Upwork.com or Iwriter.com and odesk.com for more information on becoming a Freelancer. Freelance means you work for a client on a project by project basis. You want to build a portfolio of your work as you go. You want to go over and beyond. Be clear on what you will and what you won't do. Exceed customer's expectations. Know your worth. Always work on building your platform as an expert. You want to be the very best. Learn all you can about your area of expertise. Work to improve every day. Offer a white paper of tips or an eBook of tips to help your potential clients do something they want to do. As soon you can get a website. You will also need a blog. Blog consistently.

41. Joint Venture-Joint Ventures are win-win partnerships. You can offer your products or service to this partner and he or she can do the same in return. Also you just offer your product or service to your Joint Venture Partner and give them 50% or more profits. This way you still make 50% or less that you might not have otherwise made. You will now have these customers on your list and you can sell to them in the future without having to share the profits. This is great if you are just getting starting and your Joint Venture has a big list. Make sure you offer a great Product or service and have an excellent backend set up. All this means is you will send emails to the people who bought your product and service selling to them in the future. The key here is selling them higher and higher products or services.

42. Write Report-Write a Report about something you know about but also that your target market wants to know about. Sell it for $9 or more depending on how valuable the content is. This could easily be $49 for less than 20 pages. The content has to be harder to find and valuable to your target market.

43. Google Adsense-You get paid for Ads on your website when visitors click on them. It's free to sign up. You choose the types of ads that will go on your site. You choose where they will go. You can block ads that you don't want on your site. You have to have a Google Account.

44. EBay- EBay is a great way to sell numerous products. If you buy stuff from garage sales or have a garage full of stuff you want to get rid of consider selling it on eBay. Read the terms of eBay first. Also be sure to look at what people in your categories are doing to sell their product. A good picture and a clear description is key here. You can set a price or you can allow potential customers to bid on a product.

45. Professional Development "Your income will seldom exceed your Professional Development or self-improvement. Start working on yourself. What areas can you improve? Are you a procrastinator? Do you have habits that need eliminating? What can you do today to eliminate them? Do you have your goals wrote down along with a written plan of action? What skills can you learn this year that will make you more marketable? Work on your Self Esteem. Study Goal setting and the Power of your Thoughts.

46. Audible.com-Create audio recordings (audio products) and sell on Audible.com. It is pretty quick once you have an outline. Products or usually 30 minutes or longer. Don't expect to get rich though as the amount you make on each audio download depends on the customer and the subscription level they have. This will be done through Amazon. Click on the self-publish with us at the bottom of the screen. Then click on Publish to Audio.

47. Podcast-While podcast in most cases are free. Some Businesses charge for their podcast. You can offer spots for advertisers to pay to advertise their product to your guests. You can also sell your products or services on the podcast. Just be sure to offer good content. Pat Flynn offers a great series on YouTube on creating a Podcast.

48. Lunch & Learn-Consider teaching people something of value to them (your customers) during their lunch time. I have seen people charge $19 or more for 30-40 minutes. You can repurpose this content as well. You can create an eBook from it. If you do a related series, you can turn into a Bootcamp. You can also have this content for sale on your website after the Lunch and Learn. John Maxwell does this well.

49. Networking-Build relationships. This is so important. If you want to get anywhere worthwhile good solid relationships will help take you there. Consider reading Never Eat alone.

50. WSO-Warrior Offer Forum. You can sign up for a free account. Go to https//warriorplus.com. You pay $20 to start selling your products and services. Consider observing before posting an offer. You might also want to purchase a few products before posting your product or service. Please follow their terms and agreements. You can sell your information products here. Be careful with positioning here. Seller Beware: You don't want to be known as the $7 company.

51. Email Marketing-The money is in the list. Consider offering a sign up page on your website to gather names to start building relationships with your customers. You can then start sending them emails with valuable content. You can offer tips or short videos that will help them solve their problems in some way. You can offer your Products or services on every email or every few emails. It is up to you. Be careful not to sell too much. Join the list of your competitors and see how often they try to sell you something.

52. Information Products-Information Products are super easy to make money from. They are easy to create as well. I love this one the best. All I have to do is set it and forget it. I create an information product once then I make money while I sleep. I make money for years to come. Who doesn't want that? Information products are easy to produce. Information products include but are not limited to eBooks, audio, teleseminars, boot camps, membership sites, reports, ecourses, home study courses, webinars, Mastermind groups and on and on. There is so much opportunity here. Basically you would package what you know and sell it. It's easy. Keep in mind people have different learning styles. It's best to create products in digital (such as PDF), video and audio. This will demand a higher price as well if packaged together. Of course, you can sell separately if you choose. Basically if you have an outline you could create an audio program in an hour or two. Likewise, you could convert it to an eBook. A video or webinar however takes a little more time since you will need a PowerPoint or some visuals.

53. Udemy-Udemy is a platform where you create courses of your choosing. Udemy has over 10 million students. You can price your course up to $400. There are already over 40,000 courses on Udemy. Students can learn at their own pace from any device. They have an excellent support system. If you complete your course within 60 days, Udemy will promote it for you on their Twitter account. They have thousands of followers. It is a great way to make passive income. They offer free courses on exactly how to create a course. They have courses on everything from Photography to Goal Setting. They span over 190 countries. No teaching experience required. You just have to have something to teach. They have 24/7 support. Research indicates that the market for online courses hit $56.2 billion in 2014. And it should double in 2015.

A famous Quote by Zig Ziglar is "You can have anything you want if you help enough other people get what they want."

Are you cultivating more than one stream of income?

You can make money with any of these streams of income. The key is learning and constantly applying what you learn. Be open to learn about the ones that may take you out of your comfort zone. You want to consistently get better and improve on your streams of income. You want to be persistent and take action every day no matter what. Make time to develop your skills.

I need your help. When you go to the next page, Kindle gives you an opportunity to share your thoughts and opinions through your Facebook and Twitter account. If you believe your friends and family will benefit from this book, please share your thoughts with them. You might change someone's life, and I would be eternally grateful to you.

If you feel strongly about the contributions this book made to your life, please take a few seconds to post a 5-star review on Amazon. Very few people ever leave 5-star review. So it is a big deal if you do. Writing a 5-star review is like tipping me $25. I really appreciate the gesture. I feel like a million bucks whenever I get a glowing review.

If you have any questions, you can reach me via Shondamiles@yahoo.com. I will try to respond to your questions as soon as possible. You can also connect with me on Facebook and Twitter.

For more information on Shonda Miles, go to www.shondamiles.com. Shonda Miles offers a range of Products and Services including Multiple Streams of Income-how to make money while you sleep and How to make an extra $100,000 this year.

About the Author

Shonda Miles has been self-employed for 18 years. She has owned businesses ranging from an online retail store to a Training Company.

Shonda Miles is the CEO of Shonda Miles International, a company helping organizations and individuals improve performance and achieve their goals. Shonda Miles is here to help you achieve your full potential. Her purpose is to help millions of people achieve their goals and live their God given talent.

Shonda Miles is an Author, Entrepreneur, Speaker, Personal Development Trainer, Business Consultant and Business Coach. She loves reading Nonfiction books, writing business books and shopping. Personal Development is her mission. Shonda speaks, blogs and writes about a variety of personal development topics such as Time Management, Success, Goal Setting and having a Positive Attitude.

Shonda's goal is to help others achieve the level of success they desire.

Shonda Miles is a MBA Graduate. She has several successful businesses.

Shonda Miles can be reached at info@shondamiles.com or via her website at www.shondamiles.com.

www.ingramcontent.com/pod-product-compliance
Lightning Source LLC
Chambersburg PA
CBHW070339190526
45169CB00005B/1963